→→52←←
SIMPLE WAYS
T·O·GIVE
YOUR
SPIRITUAL
LIFE A LIFT

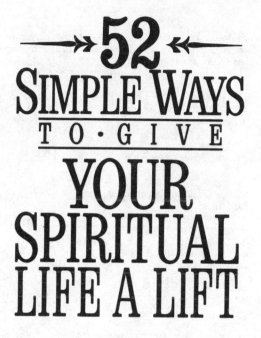

→52←
SIMPLE WAYS
TO·GIVE
YOUR SPIRITUAL LIFE A LIFT

Jan Dargatz

OLIVER NELSON

A Division of Thomas Nelson Publishers
NASHVILLE

Published in Nashville, Tennessee, by Oliver-Nelson Books, a division of Thomas Nelson, Inc., Publishers, and distributed in Canada by Lawson Falle, Ltd., Cambridge, Ontario.

Unless otherwise noted, the Bible version used in this publication is THE NEW KING JAMES VERSION. Copyright © 1979, 1980, 1982, Thomas Nelson, Inc., Publishers.

Printed in the United States of America.

Library of Congress Cataloging-in-Publication Data
Dargatz, Jan Lynette.
    52 simple ways to give your spiritual life a lift / Jan Dargatz.
        p.   cm.
    ISBN 0-8407-9602-1 (pbk.)
    1. Spiritual life.   2. Christian life—1960–   I. Title.
BV4501.2.D355   1991
248.4'6—dc20   91-22922
                                                                         CIP

1   2   3   4   5   6   —   96   95   94   93   92   91

Dedicated to

The Tuesday-Night Prayer Group

Amy
Beverly
Debbie
Diane
June
Starr
and
Suzanne

who have given my spiritual life
a lift on a weekly basis for the past seven years

Contents

WHEN THE BURDEN BECOMES TOO HEAVY TO CARRY

✳ Preface

What causes us to become down in spirit? Very often we enter a spiritually dry, drained, despairing, or depressed time because we are living at the extremes of *giving, receiving, striving,* or *carrying.*

At the extreme of *giving* we find ourselves in a position in which we have given and given and have no more to give. We feel depleted of all spiritual resources. A spiritual lift comes when we renew our capacity and desire to give and find substance worth giving.

At the extreme of *receiving* we find ourselves shut off from a source of inspiration. We have failed to feed our spirit the nourishment of the Word and to find the rest in the Lord that we need for balance, wholeness, and strength. We feel weak because we have failed to plug ourselves into the power source for our lives. A spiritual lift comes when we reestablish our relationship with the Most High God and truly "feed on him in [our] hearts by faith, with thanksgiving."*

* The Book of Common Prayer.

At the extreme of *striving* we find ourselves caught up in the spinning vortex of going, doing, meeting, accomplishing, getting, spending, racing against agendas and deadlines—we seem to be on a treadmill that won't quit. We feel detached from the higher priorities we hold to be worthy; we are too busy and too encompassed by the noise of the world to hear the still small voice of Him who speaks to us in quiet solitude. A spiritual lift comes when we shut ourselves away and listen once again with a spiritually attuned ear to what the Spirit says.

At the extreme of *carrying* we find ourselves at the end of our strength beneath the burden of worry, guilt, doubt, sorrow, frustration, or grief that has weighed down our hearts. We feel unable to carry our load—or to assist in carrying the load of another —without renewed strength. We are weary to the point of exhaustion with the problem, the frustration, the question. A spiritual lift comes when we allow the Lord not only to enter the problem but also to carry the burdensome weight of it.

In seeking a spiritual lift, we each may find it beneficial first to take a look at why we feel spiritually depressed. As any physician will tell us, the right prescription stems from a good diagnosis. In understanding something about the nature or cause of our spiritual low, we may see more clearly the way through it. This book has four major sections that address these basic conditions of spirit: "When You've Given More Than You Have to Give," "When You're Feeling Weak (Because You've Failed to Feed or Refresh Your Soul)," "When the World Is Too

Much with You (and Priorities Have Become Skewed), and "When the Burden Becomes Too Heavy to Carry." The organizational pattern of the book, however, does not restrict you from applying any one of these ways to another area of need. You may find that many or most of the ideas relate to your present state of soul.

We must also recognize at the outset of this book that no one technique or "simple way" will quickly and immediately restore us fully to the spiritual vibrancy we crave. First, the development of the soul is a process. Just as we tend to become ill in our physical bodies over time, good health is restored over time. The same holds true for our spiritual health. Although the idea that leads toward renewal may be a simple one, it will be the repeated *doing* of the idea that helps bring healing, encouragement, inspiration, renewal.

Second, no process or ritual has the capacity to heal in and of itself. Only the Lord Jesus Christ is the Healer. He alone is the Great Physician of the soul. These *52 Simple Ways to Give Your Spiritual Life a Lift* are useful only as they point us toward a deeper relationship with Him—a deeper dependency on, a deeper communion with, and a deeper understanding of the Lord and of His purposes, His methods, and His desired results in our lives. As paradoxical as the metaphors may sound, the only way to experience an ever-increasing spiritual high is to burrow deeper and deeper into His Word and His Spirit.

Finally, no "simple way" can guarantee that one will always ride on the crest of spiritual enthusiasm.

The journey toward spiritual wholeness is one that spans a lifetime and projects into eternity. Try as we might, in our human weakness we will experience detours, slowdowns, and diversions. The good news is that He is faithful to accomplish in us what He has begun! (see 1 Thess. 5:24).

When we knock, He will answer.

When we ask, He will respond.

When we seek, He will reveal.

When You've Given More Than You Have to Give

1 ✳ Retreat for a Day

Jesus, the Christ—the greatest example of sacrificial giving who has ever walked the earth—knew the value of spending time alone, of developing His inner resources to be able to give further, desire to give more, and have something worth giving to the masses that clamored for His gifts, presence, love, teachings, and miracles.

Time and again we read in the Scriptures that Jesus left the masses and went to "a deserted place by Himself" or "up on a mountain by Himself to pray" (Matt. 14:13, 23).

When you are at the end of your capacity to give, retreat. Spend a day alone. Use this time for your personal growth and development and for replenishing your resources.

Renew Your Physical Resources Without feeling strength of body, mind, and heart, it's difficult to give spiritual strength. Give *all* of your senses a rest. Turn off the television, radio, stereo, and the general noise of life—including conversations. Shut yourself away from people and the obligations of everyday life. Turn over the reins to someone else for a day!

Make your eating simple and light. Let someone wait on you. Order room service.

Go for a walk, but make it a leisurely one. Wander wherever you choose. Stop and pause as long as you like to look and listen. Take a nap. This is a day not for exertion but for relaxation.

Renew Your Mental and Emotional Resources
Surround yourself with things that are soothing and inviting to your mind. If possible, go to a place where the view and the ambience are pleasing to you, restful rather than stimulating. That place may be your own garden, a sun room, or a nearby park or gallery.

Renew Your Spiritual Resources
Spend most of your time listening to the Lord. For example, read a passage from the Gospels; then put down the Bible and meditate on what you have read. Imagine Jesus in action. How would He have spent *His* times alone in the mountains? Why did He go? Visually appraise the environment around you. Look for analogies from His words to your own life. Be open and sensitive to new insights.

Admit your weakness to the Lord in prayer. Your prayer may be just a word, a phrase, or a paragraph. This is not a day for spiritual warfare. It is a day for experiencing His love and for adoring Him in return. Listen to your own heart. Be aware of impressions you are feeling, of Scriptures you are remembering, of the silence enveloping you that seems to be pregnant with His presence.

2 ✳ Make a Joy List

Make a list of things in life that give you joy. Consider it your own private, "for my eyes only" list, and be as specific, capricious, and outrageous as you desire!

My grandmother had a favorite phrase: "That just tickles my fancy!" I still like the sound of those words. Thus, I label my list, "Things That Tickle *My* Fancy."

Favorite Things   On the list go all the things I like to see, and do, and feel, and smell, and taste, and experience.

- *Giant, clumpy snowflakes.*

- *Wet puppy kisses.*

- *My down comforter.*

- *Driving the MG on country roads with the top down and singing at the top of my lungs.*

- *A hug from six-year-old goddaughter Mary.*

- *Yellow roses.*

- *Handwritten letters that have been scented.*

- *A long lunch at my favorite restaurant with a friend.*

- *Rainy days with a good novel to read.*

- *Breakfast in bed on a Sunday morning with the newspaper funnies to read at leisure.*

- *The smell of spaghetti sauce simmering on the stove.*

- *Fireplaces to stare into.*

- *Organ postludes that fill the cathedral where I worship.*

And on and on the list goes.

Start a new list each time you're feeling worn out and world-weary.

Write and keep on writing.

Count the Joys

After you have noted at least fifty things, pause to reflect on the items you've listed. You'll no doubt come to two or three conclusions.

First, life does hold joy! As tired, shell-shocked, or spiritually exhausted as you may be, you still have the capacity to see pleasure in life!

Second, nobody else's list will read just like yours! Thank the Lord for making the things that give you joy and for giving you the unique capacity to appreciate them.

Third, your *recent* life may been void of or lacking the very things that are on your list. Decide to put some of the things on your list back into your life! Stay for the postlude; make spaghetti; get a bundle of roses; take the top off the MG; find Mary.

Delight in the Lord   Include on your list things that give you pleasure about the Lord. What about Him delights you? When have you felt joy in His presence? Perhaps your list will include one of my moments of joy in the Lord:

- The awesome quiet of His presence that overwhelms our prayer group at times.

- The sweet release I feel after times of intense prayer.

- The sound of our praise choruses filling the choir loft during prayer-and-praise services.

3 ✳ Sing a New Song

Nearly every person alive has the capacity to make a joyful noise to the Lord—to create sounds, to create tunes, and to combine them! What a high privilege to sing from the depths of our hearts to the Lord!

Find a New Song   Both the psalmist and the prophet Isaiah admonish us to sing a new song (see Ps. 33:3; Isa. 42:10). How can you do that?

Begin, perhaps, by singing songs of praise that you know. Even if the chorus or hymn is an old, familiar one, you are singing it in a new moment (that has never been lived before) or in a new circumstance (that you have never experienced before) or with a new feeling (that you have never felt before). That makes the song a *new* one!

Pick up a hymnal and find a song you've never sung before. Sing all the verses. You'll probably be amazed at the number of songs or verses in your own church hymnal that you have never heard.

Set Favorite Words to Music   Turn to the book of Psalms and use it as a source for lyrics. Give the words your own tune.

You may also want to use other passages from the

Bible, your prayer book, a favorite book of spiritual poetry, or a book of inspirational writing as a source for lyrics. Just as the Lord's Prayer can be both said and sung, so can every prayer or passage of praise in God's Word!

Make Up Your Own Song   Finally, and

perhaps most personally, give voice to your *own* prayer and praise in song. Make up your own prayers; and as you pray them, give them voice in song. Add a tune. *Your* tune. Let the music scribble across the heavens as your praise offering to God!

Sing wherever you are, no matter what you are doing. Sing honestly. Sing the true emotion you are feeling.

Singing opens the fountains of the spirit. It frees locked-in and pent-up emotions that often lurk deep in the crevices of the soul. As these spaces become free, the Holy Spirit's sweet comfort and empowering presence can, and do, come flooding in.

4 ✳ Take a Walk

Are you feeling down in spirit—as if God is far away, unconcerned about you, and unwilling or unable to carry you and your burdens in His arms?

Take a walk—a slow-paced one, a rambling one, one without time constraints.

Roam. Meander. Explore. Pause. Watch for examples of the Lord at work.

What Is God Showing You? See the Word pictures that the Lord is painting on the canvas of the world around you.

- Is a businessman napping on the park bench with his face covered by the business section of a newspaper?

- Has a weed managed to burst forth through a seemingly impenetrable layer of concrete?

- Is a grandmother exclaiming over the beauties of the park while the grandchild sleeps peacefully in her pram?

- Pause to watch the young child building one sand castle after the next—creating one and scattering it and beginning again.

- Would you have picked out that particular spot to build your nest if you were a bird?

- How many shades of green can you discern?

- Follow the trail of ants on the path before you. Watch their efforts and their progress.

- Will that piano really fit through the upstairs window as it's hoisted high above the sidewalk?

- How can snow make even a pile of trash bags look more appealing?

Seeing God at Work   The presence of God is everywhere and in all things. We can see Him there at work if we will only take the time and effort —teaching and loving and blessing and enhancing and causing life to go forward according to His purposes.

In taking a walk through God's world, we often have renewed insight into His walk through ours.

5 ✳ Surround Yourself with Beauty

In the ancient world beauty was regarded as a rare and wonderful attribute. In a world of raw odor, raucous noise, tumultuous chaos, teeming masses, unrefined natural resources, and a rarity of free-flowing water, dyes, spices, and ointments, beauty was often perceived as anything communicating peace, harmony, color, quiet, water, and a radiance of light. Beauty pertained not only to comeliness of appearance but also to peaceful serenity and inner qualities. Above all, beauty was regarded as a gift from God and, ultimately, as an attribute belonging to Him.

Described this way, beauty is perhaps no less rare in our world today!

What Beauty Does for Us   In the absence of beauty the soul is limited to that which is utilitarian. Beauty gives us a reason to go beyond the practical and useful. The beauty of holiness compels us toward the holy One. Beauty reminds us of an Eden lost and creates in us a desire for Eden restored. The apostle John saw heaven as a place of utter and indescribable beauty, replete with all that was sustaining and holy and lovely. Beauty causes us to catch a glimpse of heaven.

Often as we give to others spiritually, we can become mired in the work we do. Our vision becomes limited to what is practical, useful, and need-meeting at the basic level. We fail to regard beauty highly or to see its value—and yet it is beauty that creates in us the hope that transcends circumstances.

Find a Place of Beauty   Surround yourself with beauty today. Give your eyes, your ears, your senses—your entire being—a plunge into the beautiful. It may be—

- an hour spent in a garden or a park;

- an afternoon spent on a high hill overlooking a valley or canyon below;

- an evening at the beach watching the sun sink into the ocean;

- a quiet morning in the sanctuary of a cathedral, watching the dance of colors as the sun streams through the stained-glass windows.

Water, color, harmonious shape, quiet, plants or flowers, peaceful sounds, and meaningful symbols— these evoke a quietness of spirit, a restoration of soul, a symbolic link to the eternal Lord, the giver of life.

If you don't have a place of beauty in your life, find one or create one.

If you have one, spend time there.

Absorb the beauty. Take it in through all your

senses. Let your heart soar toward the Creator of all that is beautiful. And take with you a vivid mental image of that place to which you can retreat during busy days and tiring moments, no matter where you are.

6 ✸ Make a Thank List

Any day can be Thanksgiving Day. Even today!

The psalmist said that the appropriate way to enter the gates of God's presence is with thanksgiving (see Ps. 100:4). Thanksgiving is the *way* we come into His life-giving, need-meeting, soul-satisfying, fully restoring presence.

The Source of Thanksgiving Thanksgiving is the precursor of praise. We feel no deep need to praise the Lord for what He has done or to worship Him for who He is if we feel self-sufficient and self-reliant. From our insufficiency and utter dependency comes thankfulness for His sufficiency and sustenance. From thankfulness comes praise to Him as our Provider and Sustainer.

Even when we feel spiritually drained and exhausted—indeed, *especially* so—our thoughts toward God must begin with thanksgiving. At those times we already feel that we lack needed resources. How much greater our need to proclaim, and thus claim, His provision and His life-giving power.

Thank You, Lord . . .   One of the best ways to give thanks is to make a list of things for which you are thankful!

- Be specific and concrete. Don't generalize in the abstract. Include what you had to eat at your last meal, the clothes you are wearing now, the last person with whom you spoke.

- Be thankful for the exhaustion or sorrow you feel—that is, be thankful that the Lord has given you the capability to give, the ability and willingness to serve others, and the capacity to feel what others feel and to empathize with their needs. Choose to be thankful *in* your present circumstance or situation—thankful to the Lord that He is present in the circumstance with you and that He will see you through this "valley of the shadow of death" to a place and time of wholeness.

- Be thankful for the provision that the Lord has and will continue to have for you. Look toward the strength, health, and renewal that you will feel tomorrow as you trust the Lord to be faithful in bringing you from darkness to light, from sickness to health, from weakness to strength, from death to life everlasting, from despair to hope eternal.

From Thanksgiving to Praise   By giving thanks—and by disciplining ourselves to enumerate and itemize our thanks—we cause our minds to turn from our weakness to His strength, from our inability to His ability, from our failure to His success, and from our lack to His abundance. In doing so, we put ourselves in position for *Him* to lift us up from where we are to where He is!

7 ✸ Pamper Yourself

What would you like to give today, within the realm of your ability to give, to a person you value more than any other on earth? Think about it for a moment.

- Think about a friend who is exceedingly precious to you. Imagine that it is his or her birthday . . . or wedding day . . . or Christmas. What would your friend enjoy receiving?

- Think about the one you love. Is it your spouse? How did you court her? How did you woo her? How did you show your affection to him? How did you win his heart?

- Think about a beloved family member. What would you do if you received word that this beloved one was in a serious accident or diagnosed with a serious illness? What would you do for him or her? What would you say?

- Think about a child you love. Imagine that this child has been injured on the playground, or cruelly taunted by other children, or neglected or abused.

No doubt, your responses to these significant persons in your life would be expressions of tenderness, concern, and pampering. You would pick a bouquet of flowers, write words of encouragement and love, fix their favorite foods, hold them tight, and talk to them in affirming, soothing tones—emphasizing what is positive, good, and right about them. You'd do whatever it took to build them up on the inside and comfort them on the outside.

Do unto Yourself As You Would Do unto Others

Now put yourself into the position of that loved one. Are you feeling wounded, weak, or weary? Are you feeling unloved? Are you feeling put down, put upon, or put out?

- Send yourself a bouquet.

- Write a poem of encouragement to yourself. Paint a self-portrait in words. Remind yourself of your good points.

- Fix your favorite meal.

- Have a talk with yourself. Speak to yourself the way you would to a friend who was feeling as you are feeling!

- Let someone else touch you and hug you. There's no substitute for human touch, even if it comes in the form of a massage, a manicure, a pedicure, or a shampoo and haircut!

Love Yourself   Jesus taught, "You shall love your neighbor as yourself" (Matt. 22:39). In other words, your loving of your neighbor is only as good as the way you love yourself! If you don't value yourself, how can you value another? If you don't hold yourself in high esteem, how can you esteem someone else?

Find a way to show love to yourself today. Your capacity to love others will be renewed at the same time. Then ask the Lord to channel that love through you to do His work with renewed ability.

8 ✳ Try Chanting

Chanting?

The very word sounds foreign to our twentieth-century, Western ears. It rings of mystical, faraway rituals; offbeat theologies; or the solemn, dark halls of Gregorian friaries. Unfortunately, chanting for many people has taken on the connotation of the New Age or Eastern religions. It wasn't always so and need not be so now!

Why Chanting? Chanting, in and of itself, is a spiritual *method*. It is not a theology or a doctrine. As a method, it is subject to how we use it and why. Like all methods, it can be used for negative or positive purposes.

Many saints in the history of the Christian church have used simple, repetitive chants to focus their minds and hearts on the Lord. They have found that words and phrases spoken in chant are also a good means for bringing groups of people into unity of thought, word, and spirit. Indeed, the refrains of hymns and choruses stem from the concept of chanting.

Think of chanting as having a twofold purpose:

1. To place attention on the words that are being

spoken by a person, rather than on the person or the environment, and, through repetition, to cause one to focus on the *object* of those words even more than on the words.

2. To create a rhythmic form of communication that is as natural and harmonious as inhaling and exhaling, taking in and giving out, thinking and speaking.

Thus, when you chant a phrase, your mind turns to those words rather than to others. The more you repeat the words, the more your mind focuses on the *meaning* behind the words and not on the words themselves.

Using Chants to Focus

The following phrases are a wonderful way of focusing the heart on the Lord during personal times of prayer and meditation.

"Father, I love You."

"Thank You, O Lord."

"Praise to You, O Lord Most High."

"Almighty Father, I give You my life [time, hurt, want, love]."

Chanting can be a useful way to shut off and put out of our minds the thoughts, the impressions, and even the awareness of the outside world.

9 ✸ Play!

How sad that many adults have lost the ability to play. Oh, we spend the weekend at the lake under the guise of recreation or relaxation—but are we really playing?

Hallmarks of True Play

- *Free-form movement from activity to activity without an agenda.*

- *Laughter.*

- *Intrinsic reward.*

- *Worry-free sense of safety.*

What a far cry these characteristics of play are from a fishing trip with quotas, a four-hour timetable for a visit to the amusement park, or a recreational weekend with access to a telephone and a preoccupation with a briefcase full of work!

Jesus admonished His followers—including us—to become like little children. Certainly, one of the foremost childlike attributes is that of play!

Allow Yourself to Play in the Lord's Presence Today

- Do something that causes you to laugh.

- Spend an afternoon without a list of things to do. Do what you *feel* like doing.

- Pack a picnic lunch, call a friend, and get in the car and drive.

- Recall what gave you pleasure as a child and try one of those activities.

As You Play . . .

- Refuse to think about or talk about work. Turn your conversations to dreams, imaginings, and discussions of other issues.

- Avoid the tendency to talk about the fact that you *are* playing. Just play!

Spiritual Benefits of Play   Play does three things for us spiritually.

1. It neutralizes our preoccupation with work, including our ministry, which often takes on the qualities of work (with agendas, goals, timetables, and job descriptions).

2. Play helps us shift gears physically and emotionally.

3. Finally, play truly happens only when we cast all of our worry on the Lord.

10 ✳ Fill Your World with Praise Music

Don't feel like praising? Too cast down or spiritually tired to think about praising the Lord? Too weary or battered spiritually to give thanks?

Create an environment that will build up your spirit so that you desire to and are able to praise the Lord. How? By surrounding yourself with praise music!

Play it in your car. Fill your house with it. Carry it with you as you jog or go for a walk in the park.

Explore the Possibilities

- Find a Christian radio station that you enjoy and set your car radio to it.

- Go to a Christian bookstore and discover today's artists and groups.

- Rediscover the old hymns and traditional songs of the church.

- Try new selections.

What Praise Music Can Do   Have you ever primed a water pump? Putting a little water into the pump system causes the mechanism to pump up the deep waters of the earth.

Praise music works the same way. The praise you feel for the Lord really is there—although it may be concealed by the debris of concern, the pipes of the pump may have become corroded, or the water table of your heart may have dropped in the drought of spiritually dry times. Hearing praise music eventually causes your own praise to *want* to come forth.

Have you ever caught yourself tapping your toes to a rousing barn-dance jig or singing along when you hear a familiar song from your teenage years? Praise music can cause the toes of your soul to dance involuntarily. It can prompt you to sing along without forethought.

Don't Be Surprised—

- when you find yourself joining with someone else's words of praise:

- when you find yourself humming or singing a tune later:

- when you once again *want* to voice your thanksgiving and praise to the Lord.

Listening to praise music allows the Word of God—in song—to reenter your heart. It allows another brother or sister in Christ to teach you and encourage you in song. It allows the work of the Lord to be done in your life!

11 ❋ Spend Time Observing a Child

Children are great teachers. Too often, however, we miss the lessons they have to offer us because we fail to attend the "classes" they are conducting!

Take time out of your schedule to observe children—not to baby-sit, play, or instruct but simply to observe. Set aside your preconceived ideas about children. Don't look for evidence to support your favorite theories. Just *watch*.

Notice How Children Relate to Those in Authority over Them

- What happens during arguments?
- What happens after punishment?
- What happens under leadership?
- What requires leadership?
- What doesn't require leadership?

Watch How Children Relate to One Another

- What is the dynamic among children of like age, size, sex, ability, or ethnic background?

- What happens when children differ in age, height, sex, levels of skill, or ethnic background?

- What is the difference between two children at play and a dozen children at play?

- What happens to create competition, during competition, and after competition?

- What are the dynamics of cooperation?

- What is the difference between children who know each other well and those who don't?

Evaluate How Children Relate to Their Environment

- When are they comfortable? How do you know? What causes them to become uncomfortable? What do they do in times of discomfort?

- What environments do children create? How? For what purposes?

- What compels their curiosity? What is boring?

Observe How Children Relate to Time

- Does time matter? Why or why not?

- How do children react when time is up?

Appraise the Difference between Work and Play   Is there one? What are the distinguishing characteristics? Observe what happens when play is dictated and when it is forbidden.

Study How Children Exhibit Values
Note the way children display concepts adults hold to be valuable: trust . . . hope . . . honesty . . . reality . . . friendship.

Observe Emotional Responses   What does a child do when he becomes discouraged . . . weary . . . troubled . . . frustrated?

Watch and Learn!   Most of us who observe children with an open mind and, more importantly, with an open and spiritually attuned heart, learn valuable lessons about growth, patience, persistence, rest, relationship, time, control, and ways to turn play into work and work into play. We learn more about what it really means to trust, receive, and follow.

12 ✴ Spend a Weekend at a Monastery

Many people think of monasteries and convents as belonging to faraway places or times. We often think of them as being inaccessible, remote, foreign, and off-limits. The opposite is more likely true.

A Spiritual Retreat Many monasteries and convents provide on a regular basis a haven of rest for weary travelers on the faith road. Some accommodate visitors for weekends, overnight stays, short-term stays, or specified quiet days and seminars.

A weekend or even an overnight stay alone at a monastery can be a wonderful opportunity for recovering a feeling of spiritual strength, balance, and joy. Such a weekend can provide prolonged sessions of meditation and prayer that nurture the soul. Such a weekend can help immensely in reestablishing disciplines and priorities you hold valuable.

What You Can Expect

- *Be prepared to adopt the monastery or convent's rule of life.* These places aren't spas or resorts. They are communities in which work is done— both practical and spiritual. Don't go unless you are willing to adjust to the rules and schedule. Don't expect anyone to adjust to you, wait on you, be available to you, or solve your problems. You can expect a quiet and supportive environment in which you can sort out your own inner business.

- *Be prepared to enjoy quiet hours, with few amenities.* You'll spend most of your time alone, which is great if you are seeking quiet for meditation, reading, or prayer.

- *Be prepared for an inner journey.* You'll feel support and camaraderie in the faith, but don't expect advice, counseling, therapy, or medical help.

- *Be prepared to support the work of the community with a financial gift.* Flat fees are rarely posted. Offerings are always accepted. Be generous. Giving is part of the experience.

- *Be prepared for God to meet you there.* Ask Him to do so. Expect Him to. Look for ways in which He does.

13 ✳ Praise Him!

All of the suggestions in this section of the book have had one goal: to bring you to a point that you *want* to praise and worship the Lord and actually do so.

Themes of Praise

- *Praise God for what He has done for you.* Consider your past and praise the Lord for the ways He has provided for you and has led you. Consider the people, incidents, and circumstances He has used to mold you more and more into the likeness of His Son, Jesus Christ, and to the fullness of your own potential.

- *Praise Him for all the resources He has placed at your disposal.* Praise Him for His creation and your participation in it!

- *Praise Him for the relationships you hold dear.* Consider the people whom He has brought across your life's path. Praise Him for the lives of those who have loved you, taught you, nurtured you, and disciplined you. Praise Him for the privilege you enjoy of belonging to His vast and eternal family.

- *Praise Him for His plan*—for sending His Son to redeem your life—and for the work He is calling you to do for the redemption of others.

- *Praise Him, above all, for who He is.* Recall the many names of God, Jesus, and the Holy Spirit through the Scriptures (there are more than seven hundred!). List them. Meditate on them.

Why Praise?   Because praise is the ultimate key for renewing your spirit. It puts everything back into perspective.

- You are the created; He is Creator.

- You are the clay; He is the Potter.

- You are the child; He is the Father.

- You are the finite one in wisdom, strength, and time. He is the infinite One—omniscient, omnipotent, and omnipresent.

By admitting your weakness, you are in the correct position to receive His strength.

When You're Feeling Weak

(Because You've Failed to
Feed or Refresh Your Soul)

14 ✳ Seek Out a Local Church Where You Can Give and Receive

When we fail to eat and exercise, we become physically weak. The same is true for the spirit. In order to become and remain spiritually strong, we must provide our souls with proper nutrients and opportunities for exercise.

Get Involved   Find a place where you can and will participate regularly and frequently. Strive for *consistent* participation in church services and events. The regularity of hearing God's Word . . . singing with God's people . . . giving to God's work . . . and partaking in holy Communion and other meaningful rituals of the church all work together to create a sense of community and corporate strength.

Don't just attend church. Get involved. Find a means of giving—of sharing what you have inside you. Build relationships. Then, when you are feeling weak, you can let the strength of others bolster you and buoy you up! Let the church be your first resort and your foremost support group in times of crisis or weakness.

Make a commitment to learn the needs of those

you worship alongside and to meet their needs to the best of your ability. Admit your weaknesses to others and receive their help. Pray for others and allow them to pray for you in return.

15 ✸ Avail Yourself of Anointed Preaching

My grandmother defined *anointed preaching* this way: *"Regular* preaching is when the preacher says nice-sounding words that make me pleased with myself. *Anointed* preaching is when the preacher says words that make me displeased with the present state of my soul so that I feel a need for more of God."

Throughout the Scriptures an anointing by oil symbolized the Holy Spirit's being poured on, or into, a person's life. In anointed preaching the Holy Spirit pours Himself into our lives through messages about Jesus Christ.

Seek Out Anointed Preaching

- Anointed preaching can be heard from the pulpit and at evangelistic rallies, citywide services, seminars, conferences, and other meetings.

- Anointed preaching is available in abundance on audiocassette tapes and videotapes.

- Anointed preaching is heard on many Christian radio and television programs.

- Some of the powerful sermons preached early in our nation's history are available from the library.

- The preaching of Jesus and Paul and others can be "heard." Read aloud the Sermon on the Mount and the parables of Jesus. Read the sermons of Peter and Paul in the book of Acts. Read aloud the letters of Paul, John, James, and Peter in the New Testament—letters that were actually read aloud, in most cases, as "sermons" to the early Christian believers.

Do Your Part

1. Before you hear or read a sermon, pray that the Holy Spirit will open the ears of your spirit to hear the message He has for you.

2. As you hear a sermon, continually look for points that are applicable to your present circumstances in life. Don't assume that the words are for someone else. Assume that they are for *you* and that *you* need to hear them.

3. After you've heard a sermon, thank God for what you've heard and ask Him never to let you forget it. Look for ways to live that message in your everyday life.

4. Finally, tell someone else within twenty-four hours what you've heard or read. The repreaching of God's Word will reinforce it for you and will help you remember and apply it. It will also bless someone else!

16 ✳ Establish a Daily Discipline of Reading God's Word and of Praying

Make prayer and Bible reading daily habits. Establish them as unshakable disciplines in your life.

Give Them First Priority Most Christians with whom I've discussed these daily disciplines agree: early morning is the best time for prayer and Bible reading. Why? Because your mind is less distracted then; you're free from the clutter and problems of the day's agenda. You're also the most alert and refreshed physically, mentally, and emotionally. Furthermore, as you literally establish reading God's Word and communicating with Him as your first priority, your desire that He be your first priority *spiritually* becomes more clearly established. There's a greater likelihood that you will recall throughout the day what you have read and said that morning and will use it more readily.

You certainly don't have to limit your Bible reading and prayer discipline to the morning hours. Some people find great solace in taking a noonday break.

A Daily Appointment   A number of years ago when I was in my early teens, a missionary to Samoa came to my Sunday school class and said, "Read your Bible every day. Read it until you read something that you know is God's word directly to you. Pray every day. Pray until you weep for lost souls." It is the best approach to daily Bible reading and prayer I've ever heard.

Our need for spiritual strength comes daily. Problems strike unexpectedly. Situations change overnight. Our battle with the enemy of our souls is a constant one. Therefore, reinforcing and building up both our offensive and defensive spiritual capabilities must take place on a daily basis. Why pray and read daily? Because we *need* to.

Many people floss their teeth with greater regularity than they read God's Word. Many talk to their dogs or cats more than they talk to God. Don't be among them. Draw strength from a living, daily relationship with the Source of all strength—your almighty Father in heaven.

17 ✳ Attend a Special Church Service

Are you feeling undernourished spiritually? Try adding a special time of worship to your weekly schedule.

Special Services

- A midweek service.

- A Sunday school class.

- Vespers or a Sunday-evening service.

- An evening prayer service, a Bible study, or a Christ-centered share group once a week.

- A prayer group or a prayer-and-praise fellowship that meets regularly.

Expanding the Possibilities   The "service" may be one in which you share vicariously.

- You may choose to view faithfully one videotape in a Bible-study series each week until you have seen the entire series.

• Or you may choose to listen faithfully to at least one audiocassette a week in a preaching series.

The "service" may be more academic than inspirational. You may choose to enroll in a longer course, such as a Bible course offered by a Christian college, or a Bible-study series (such as Kerygma or Precepts), or a training program in a specific area of ministry.

The "service" may actually be a concentrated *series* of services conducted as a special conference, seminar, or crusade.

You may find that a Communion service provides the spiritual refreshment for which your soul has been aching. How long has it been since you sat at table with the Lord and with others of like faith? When was the last time you accepted the body and blood of our Lord Jesus Christ as your own?

The services of the church are all ultimately designed for meeting spiritual needs. That was their initial reason for being! Avail yourself of the opportunities they offer to experience healing, restoration, and strength.

18 ✻ Read the Bible for Five Minutes

A person who is near starvation cannot enjoy a banquet feast. He can eat only a few bites at a time. A person who has been without water for several days can take only small sips from a canteen.

The same principle holds true for those who have been away from the nourishing power of God's Word for some time . . . those who have been tremendously overwhelmed or overcome by a crisis or tragedy . . . and those who have never before read the Bible for themselves!

If one of these situations applies to you . . .

Follow These Steps

1. Pick up your Bible and read it for just five minutes at a time. Do this as many times during the day as you feel the need for God's Word and whenever you are feeling the onset of anxiety, fear, doubt, nervousness, or frustration.

2. Begin in the Gospels, especially with Mark and Luke. Read the stories about Jesus. (They are the easiest passages of the Bible to understand and on which to concentrate.)

3. Choose a Bible that is written in language that is easy to understand. Try the *New King James Version,*

The Living Bible, the *New International Verson,* or the *Good News Bible.* If you've never read the Bible before, you may even want to begin with a children's Bible storybook to become acquainted with the Bible stories.

4. Before you begin reading, pray this brief prayer: "Heavenly Father, help me to understand what I am about to read."

5. Read aloud. It will help you concentrate on and comprehend the meaning of the passage.

6. If you read a sentence and don't seem to comprehend it, read it again. You may find yourself reading and rereading one paragraph for the entire five minutes. That's OK! Let those words soak into your parched soul.

7. When you finish reading, pray again, "Heavenly Father, help me to remember what I have just read and to put it to work in my life."

You Can Always Take Five Minutes Out of a Schedule!

Take your Bible with you so you can read it periodically throughout the day wherever you go. These five-minute feedings are to your spirit what a bottle of nourishment is to a newborn infant. They will bring life back to your spirit. They will begin to establish a new pattern of faith and trust to replace fear and doubt. They will refocus your attention from the cares of the world to the eternal purposes and plan of God. These small passages of Scripture, over time, will be knit together by the Holy Spirit to create a new fabric of soul.

19 ✳ Pray Your Own Rosary

A few years ago I decided to purchase a rosary. I chose a child's rosary—with bright, big wooden beads and a bold red cross. I read the simple instructional booklet that came with it and followed the litany prescribed. I candidly admit that the prayers meant very little to me, although I believe that they are meaningful to many people who recite them. I chose instead to use my rosary in a different way.

A Tool for Prayer   I devote the small beads of my rosary to those I want to remember in prayer on a daily basis. There are fifty small beads in a rosary, divided into five sections. I assign one section each to family, personal friends, fellow parishioners, work associates, and those with whom I'm presently working on projects or committees. It's easy to think of at least ten persons a day in each area—and they aren't always the same persons each day. I use the five large beads separating these sections as a time for prayer about personal needs in my life. I allocate the cross for the Lord's Prayer and the remaining four beads for a season of praise, a season of worship, the beatitudes recited in the form of a prayer, and a prayer for the peace of Jerusalem. Thus, my rosary is my tool for prayer.

The Value of a Rosary

1. *It calls my remembrance to individual persons.* I don't pray for categories or generalities. I pray for specifics and for individual loved ones and associates whom I call by name.

2. *The rosary provides for me a very real image that I am touching these persons in prayer.* As my fingers hold each bead, I feel as if I am actually touching each person spiritually.

3. *The rosary provides me a framework for persistent prayer.* I have come again and again before the Lord with my deep, heartfelt concerns for some of the individuals on my rosary.

4. *The rosary is a picture to me of the way lives are linked together in Christ Jesus.* No person is isolated from those on either side of him. We are connected as believers in the Lord.

It's wonderful to be able to touch, remember, individualize, and conceptualize one's role as a member of the body of Christ. My bulky, colorful, wooden child's rosary helps *me* do that. Praying in this way helps you feel intimately attached to the Lord and His people. In that you will discover nourishment and strength for your soul.

20 ✳ Read the Life Stories of the Saints

When we feel as if we are spiritually at the end of the road and out of fuel, the *last* thing any of us probably feels like is the very thing that most of us ultimately desire to be—a saint of God!

Meet the Saints One of the best ways to give your life a spiritual lift is to read the biographies of the saints through the history of the church.

- Get acquainted with Augustine, Agnes, Frances, Benedict, Clare.

- Meet Thomas Aquinas, John Chrysostom, Patrick, Aidan, and Catherine of Siena.

- Read about Clement, Hilda, Nicholas.

- Read the life stories of the Gospel writers— Matthew, Mark, Luke, John. Read the stories of Peter and Paul.

- Read the biographies of those who have founded some of the major denominations: John and Charles Wesley, Martin Luther, John Calvin, Aimee Semple McPherson.

- Read the biographies of famous recent-history evangelists and leaders in the church: Charles Spurgeon, Billy Graham, Oral Roberts, Billy Sunday.

- Read the stories of missionaries like David Livingstone.

Learn from the Saints   Reading the lives of the saints will make you realize that every human being has frailties and emotional highs and lows. Reading the lives of the saints will give you insight into the redemptive work of God—and His ability to root out all sins; compensate for all weaknesses and inabilities; and conquer all adversities, sicknesses, or trials.

21 ✳ Take a Daily Excursion into the Psalms and Proverbs

Two books of the Bible seem especially suitable for once-a-month reading: Proverbs and Psalms.

Be Systematic   Proverbs defines in detail the essentials for godly interpersonal relationships. The book has thirty-one chapters. Read one every day of the month. (In months with fewer than thirty-one days, expand your reading on the last day of the month.)

Psalms depicts the ideal relationship between God and persons. The book has 150 chapters or songs. Read five a day for a month. (In months with thirty-one days, pick out a few of your favorites to reread.) You might also consider reading the psalms on a one-a-day basis, thereby reading them all in the course of five months.

Repeat your reading of Proverbs and Psalms month after month. Let their words and concepts sink deep into your heart and soul.

Apply Their Truths   Continually be on the alert for examples from your life that relate to Proverbs. Ask the Lord to quicken His principles to your mind as you go about your daily chores and schedule and to show you how to apply the commandments in Proverbs to your business, career, or immediate task or job; to your marriage; and to your children.

Before going to sleep each night, meditate on what you remember reading from the book of Proverbs. Dwell on the foremost concept you recall.

Consider making Proverbs and Psalms the core of a daily-Bible-reading program that you establish with your child.

Always Something New   No matter how many times you read Proverbs and Psalms, you'll continually find something new and fresh about them. Enjoy the never-ending richness of God's Word to you—its ever-new applications and always-inspiring revelations.

A daily reading of Proverbs and Psalms in these ways can give you a practical handle to grasp in furthering your spiritual development. These books provide for you a very specific and easy-to-follow curriculum for enriching your soul and for giving your spiritual life a lift.

22 ✳ Testify on Behalf of the Lord

A challenge for every Christian is to be a witness to the power and working of the Lord God on the earth today.

What Does a Witness Tell? What he has seen, heard, and knows to be true. We've all seen reenactments of an eyewitness's testimony in a courtroom. A witness in the courts of the United States of America swears to tell the whole truth and nothing but the truth, by God's help.

Similarly, we are called to tell everything we know about the Lord, to rely on God's help in the process, and to report accurately only what we know to be true about Him—not what we have surmised or learned secondhand but what we have experienced in our own lives. We're both responsible for doing that work and privileged to do so.

Therefore, find occasion to recall the blessings of the Lord that you have personally experienced!

Share Your Experiences Consider sharing your experiences with members of your family, especially your children. Relate incidents in your life in which you have experienced personally the power, prompting, or presence of the Lord. This sharing will give your family new insight into you and a practical understanding of how God works in and through individuals.

If you feel that your experiences will help others grow in their faith, share them in your conversations.

What Your Testimony Can Do   What has the Lord Jesus Christ done for you? What does He mean to you? Tell it.

In giving a testimony, you do two things:

1. You remind yourself of God's blessings. As you hear your own story, your faith is renewed.

2. You extend the kingdom of God by adding to the body of evidence that the Holy Spirit is amassing in someone's life to woo him to the Lord, to convict him to repentance, or to confirm God's Word to him.

Your testimony is evidence of God's life-changing power and life-indwelling presence. In the telling are renewal and refreshment—for you and for others.

Want a spiritually uplifting experience? Talk about Jesus, the One who spiritually uplifts!

23 ✳ Soak Up the Word of God

Time and again the holy Scriptures tell us that the commandments of the Lord in the Word of God are life-giving. The Scriptures promote growth. They stimulate expansion. They cause multiplication. They renew and restore. They cause new birth spiritually. They create.

Become a Student of the Word Set out on a personal Bible study. You may want to focus on:

- *The life story of an individual,* such as Abraham, Moses, Ruth, or Paul. Above all, be acquainted with the life and words of Jesus.

- *Concepts and symbols.* Pick one and, using a concordance, look up all passages related to it. Make notes of the insights you draw from each reference. (Try starting with the concepts of *cup, fruit,* or *hand.*)

- *One book of the Bible.* Consult as many commentaries and reference materials as you can to gain insight into the book's author, purpose, composition, and message.

- *A series of books,* such as the Penteteuch (the first five books of the Bible), the Wisdom Literature (Psalms, Proverbs, Ecclesiastes, and Song of Solomon), the Prophets, the history books, the Gospels, the letters of Paul, the letters of Peter, or the letters of John.

- *One topic of interest*—for example, all the Bible says about children; the Old Testament prophecies that relate to the life of Jesus: or word pictures painted by Bible references to animals, birds, and plants.

Rich Rewards   An in-depth study of God's Word over the years will bring you to a new level of understanding of God's overall plan for humankind and of the ways He works in the hearts of individuals. You'll see your life in the context of His whole. You'll have revelations and insights into His purposes—the whys of His actions and the desires of His heart.

When the World Is Too Much with You

(and Priorities Have Become Skewed)

24 ✳ Get Out of Debt

In an age of upwardly spiraling debt, the gaping jaws of financial doom seem to be snapping at us from all sides. Perhaps more than ever before, the words of the Apostle Paul both convict and challenge: "Owe no one anything except to love one another" (Romans 13:8).

Getting out of debt generally involves three significant (sometimes radical) changes in one's life.

- *Vastly reduce the level of want.* A general rule of thumb seems to be: "shop less, spend less." Try staying out of the malls, leaving the mail-order catalogs unopened, and turning off the shopping channel.

- *Find new ways of meeting needs.* Be creative in this area! Clipping coupons may not be for you; you may prefer carpooling, discount shopping, or a less expensive vacation alternative.

- *Choose to be accountable.* Regularly take stock of your finances. Check your spending against a budget and balance your checkbook monthly; discuss spending with your spouse in an organized facts-oriented manner; establish a reward system for good performance.

Get Help for Sick Finances   If your finances seem hopelessly sick, find someone who is a certified financial planner or work with someone at a reputable lending institution.

- *Pay cash.* Use credit cards only for emergency or travel purposes; if you find yourself in a pattern of not being able to pay the outstanding balance on a monthly basis, put your credit cards away—and, better yet, cut them up.

- *Establish a reasonable budget.* Seek out ways for increasing your income and decreasing your spending. Set interim goals. When you get one account paid in full, use that money to double-up your payments on a second account.

- *Save something and give something every month.* Even if you put only $5 a week into a savings account, at the end of a year—given a reasonable rate of interest that compounds quarterly— you'll have nearly $275!

When you are in debt, your resources are *not* your own. A part of them belongs, by your mutual agreement, to someone else.

When you are in debt, your ability to prioritize your spending is *not* your own. Creditors take first priority.

When you are in debt, your time and mobility ultimately are not your own. You *must* work and earn to pay those from whom you have borrowed.

25 ✳ Regroup with Your Christian Friends

Spend time with your Christian friends and family members! Nurture your relationships with them as your Christian sisters and brothers. Share your heart with them. Learn from them. Have fun with them. Give to them and receive from them. After all, you'll be spending eternity with them!

Invest in People The only potentially lasting thing you can touch on this earth is the life of another person. Only human beings have the capacity for and destiny of eternity.

Therefore, choose to be with your Christian sisters and brothers. Make time to be with them. Establish your relationships with them as a priority.

Should we limit our associations to Christians? Certainly not. Jesus spent a great deal of His time with masses who were hearing His message for the first time or who had not yet accepted His message fully. Still, when the time came for Jesus to take comfort in human contact, He turned to those closest to Him in spirit. They became His family (see Matt. 12:46–50).

Therefore . . .

- Don't assume that your Christian friends will understand your absence or your neglect. Spend time with them. Be available not only when you need them but also when they need you.

- Don't take your Christian friends for granted. Rather, treat them with the utmost preference and respect. Apologize to them when you need to. Accommodate them and forgive them. Love them generously.

Are you feeling caught up in the dizzying spin of too many tasks?

Call a Christian friend and make a date.

26 ❋ Talk About Heaven

There's nothing like a good, in-depth conversation about heaven to restore your sense of priorities and to give perspective to your current crisis!

Endless Possibilities Spend some time with your Christian friends letting your spiritual imaginations run wild as you talk about heaven.

- What will you be doing there? Is it possible that God will send you on special missions to other planets and faraway galaxies?

- Whom will you meet there? With which follower of the Lord can you hardly wait to spend time? What will you discuss? Explore what it will be like to live with others in a completely harmonious atmosphere of love, compatibility, and mutuality of purpose.

- What will you learn in heaven? What are the foremost questions you'll ask of the Lord?

- How will you feel there? What will it be like to have no limitations on your ability to move, sense, experience, or think?

- How will you live there? In which neighborhood, surrounded by what things, and for what purpose will you have those things?

The possibilities are endless—because heaven is a place of endless possibilities!

A discussion about heaven most certainly involves a discussion of eternity. Explore the idea that no mathematical equation can compare the time we have on earth with the unlimited time of eternity. Imagine what it will be like to live without clocks, schedules, deadlines, and delays.

Purposeful Imaginings   A discussion of heaven can do three things for you.

- It can put your priorities in order. Only certain things count toward eternity. Focus on them.

- It can give you renewed insight into how we Christians are to bring heaven to earth and what it really means to pray,

    "Your kingdom come.
    Your will be done
    On earth as it is in heaven (Matt. 6:10).

- It can ease the urgency we often feel in seeing certain changes brought about or decisions reached in our relationships with others. God has a much broader view of time than we do. Relax and give God time to work things out.

Death will be but a transitional moment—not a true end or beginning but simply a move to the next phase of our eternal life in Jesus Christ.

The apostle Paul spoke of the "hope of eternal life" (Titus 3:7). A discussion about heaven renews that hope within us—and gives us a spiritual lift that's virtually unmatchable!

27 ✴ Start Your Day by Greeting the Lord—and End It by Thanking Him

What are the first words out of your mouth each morning? As a friend of mine asks, "Do you start your day by saying, 'Good Lord, it's morning' or by saying, 'Good morning, Lord'?"

Greetings in the Morning   Make your first words of the morning a greeting to the Lord.

- "Thank You, Lord, for another day to love You and serve You."
- "I'm trusting You, Lord, to help me live this day with grace and purpose."
- "Good morning, Lord. What would you like for me to do for You today?"
- "Thank You for such a wonderful day, heavenly Father. Show me how to make the most of it for Your kingdom."

- "I'm trusting You to be by my side every hour of this day, Lord."

When we greet the Lord as our first priority in the morning, we are saying to Him and to ourselves, "I want to be with You. I want to be found by You and sustained by You this day."

Thanksgiving at Night   According to the Jewish concept of a day, a new day begins at sunset. The Jewish day *begins* with rest in the Lord. Take time to greet the Lord at the end of your day and recognize that as you do, you are speaking to Him in anticipation of your next day on this earth!

- "Good night, Lord. As I sleep, I trust You to cleanse me of the spiritual dust that I've accumulated today. Heal me of the wounds I've experienced. Prepare me and strengthen me for the work You still have ahead for me to do."

- "I trust You, Lord, to edit what I have said and done this day to be in keeping with Your desires and Your plan for my life and for the lives of others I've touched."

- "As I prepare to sleep, Lord, cleanse the thoughts of my mind by the inspiration of Your Holy Spirit and awaken me with a renewed desire to do Your will with gladness and singularity of heart."

- "Be with me, Lord, in the night."

Frame your day—beginning and ending—with the Lord. You'll no doubt find yourself relaxing a little in the flow of life, experiencing greater peace and a deeper level of trust. And in that there's a spiritual lift for your life!

28 ✸ Read the Promises of the Bible

The Bible is filled with promises from cover to cover. Seek them out. Read them thoroughly, repeatedly, and often. Accept them as God's promises for *you*. Expect God to do what He has promised in *your* life.

The Nature of God's Promises   As you read God's promises to you, you'll no doubt discover that most of them are conditional. They are "if, then" statements promising that God *will* act as we fulfill certain obligations or enter certain commitments.

Furthermore, God doesn't promise to do our part of the equation. He will enable us or help us to do our part if we ask Him, but He will not overstep our will or neutralize the necessity of our taking action.

God's Promises for You   In reading and studying God's promises, you'll no doubt come to several conclusions about God's desires for you.

- He wants a relationship with you. He wants to call you His daughter or son, and He wants to live with you forever.

- He wants only what is good for you. He seeks your highest good. And He alone knows what that is and how to bring it about in the fullness of His timing.

• He longs for you to seek Him out, to ask of Him, and to believe Him for answers.

Build your own record of Bible promises as you read and study the Bible, highlighting certain Scriptures or keeping a running list at the back of your Bible. You may want to focus on Bible promises as a topic for personal, in-depth Bible study.

"If, Then"   The "if" part of Bible promises shows us what God wants our priorities to be. They are, as a composite, God's agenda for our lives. In accepting His agenda, we experience a spiritual lift in our lives because we no longer have to wonder, grope about, or spend time and energy struggling to discover God's will for us. His will is to do the "if" part of the Bible-promise equations!

The "then" part of Bible promises holds out wonderful rewards for us. They are God's blessings to us. As we accept His goodness to us by faith, He *does* lift us up in spirit and in reality.

The promises of God in the Bible call for us to put ourselves in a position to be lifted up easily by our heavenly Father. When we do, He does.

29 ✳ Audit Your Language

Conduct an audit of your own language on any given day, keeping track of . . .

- How many times you acknowledge the Lord.

- How many times you use swear words or slang expressions that degrade the Lord or downgrade your Christian witness.

- How many times you've taken a positive approach to a situation in your statements.

- How many times you've taken a negative approach to a problem or a challenge.

- How many times you've spoken positively about a person.

- How many times you've spoken negatively about a person.

What Does Your Audit Reveal?   Are you positively positioned or negatively positioned toward life? Do you expect God to work through people for good, or do you look for the worst in and from people?

Your words reflect the state of your heart toward God. An audit of your language is an audit of your relationship with God. Such an audit can reveal your bitterness against the deeds of others, your resentment against circumstances and situations, your level of hatred toward others. Such an audit reveals a need for repentance and can bring us to a turnaround point in our lives.

How to Do an Audit

1. Be aware of your words. Ask the Holy Spirit to prick your conscience each time you speak negatively.

2. When you speak negatively, immediately ask forgiveness of those who may have heard you and issue a positive statement.

3. Ask others around you to help you guard your language and change your speech patterns.

4. Ask the Holy Spirit to forgive you, to help you view others in a positive light, and to implement a change of heart in the way you speak.

Choose Your Words   A positive statement propels hope toward a better future, it builds up your faith and that of others, and it promotes change. Choosing to be up in the words you speak can help you feel up in spirit.

30 ✳ Write a Note of Encouragement

When the world is pressing in on you from all sides and you feel as if you are out of time, out of strength, and out of the ability to care, sit down, push away all other projects and responsibilities, and take three minutes to write a note of encouragement to someone.

Writing Your Note   Your note does not need to be long, perhaps only three or four sentences.

- Let the person know that you are thinking of her and care about her.

- Give the person an encouraging word of praise.

- State your hope—indeed, belief—that something positive will happen in his life.

Sample Notes

- "Hi! Just a note to say that I'm thinking about you and praying for you today. I believe in the work you are doing as [*position or role*], and I

support you in it. May God give you health,
strength, and wisdom as you trust Him in your
work."

• "I just heard about [*loss, illness, or accident*], and
I want you to know that I am deeply sorry and
that I'm praying for God to give you the
strength you need. You are precious to Him and
to me! I believe that the Lord can turn even this
situation into something good. I'm standing with
you in His love."

• "Just a note, [*give name*], to let you know that I
appreciate the excellent work that you do as
[*state position or role*]. You are an inspiration to
me. I believe that God will greatly use you to
advance His kingdom."

• "A little note to say that I'm so glad I'm related
to you [*or know you; state basis for relationship*].
You are an inspiration to me in so many ways,
although I rarely take the time to tell you so. I
believe that God has great blessings for you today and every day. I'm praying for you!"

• "I realize that these are difficult days for you,
but I want you to know that someone is praying
for you and is believing that God has something
good ahead for you. Don't give up. Hold out for
His best!"

• "I'm praying today specifically that God will
[*state what you believe God will do on the person's*

behalf]. I believe with all my heart that God desires to bless you in this way.

Wouldn't *you* like to receive a note like that today? Jesus taught that as we give, we receive.

31 ✳ Declare a Quiet Day in Your Life

Turn off the volume of the world for a day. See what a difference quietness can make. It's really no wonder that peace is linked with quiet in the common phrase "peace and quiet." Peace demands quiet; quiet can produce peace.

Shhh. Make it a new hallmark word for your life!

Combat the Assault on Your Senses

Noise is tiring. Clatter and chatter are exhausting. Even the constant din of nonoffensive music or media programs can be debilitating.

Your spiritual exhaustion may stem from a nonstop assault on your senses (especially hearing). After all, one of the foremost ways to sap the morale of an enemy force is to force it to experience the nonstop din of artillery fire or exploding bombs.

So . . .

- Shut off the television set. You can live without it for twenty-four hours.

- Switch off the radio in your car.

- *Don't* turn on the stereo.

- Leave your headset at home when you jog or walk.

- Limit your conversations with others. (Unplug the phone.)

- Stay away from noisy crowds.

- Deliberately avoid conversations and meetings as much as possible.

- Don't even talk aloud to yourself!

Pursue Peace   Recognize that establishing an atmosphere of quiet calm in our present society takes deliberate effort. It won't just happen. You'll have to make it happen.

If you need to get away from a noisy environment in order to experience quiet, do so! A day or two away—with as much silence as possible—can do wonders for restoring a deep feeling of peace.

Turning up your spiritual sense of well-being may involve turning down the sound level of your life!

32 ✳ Subtract One

Most of us accept too many responsibilities, juggle too many chores, have too many things to do, and attempt to sustain too many relationships. We are knee-deep in activities that are totally of our own choosing; in many cases, the Lord really hasn't asked us to do them or to be a part of them. No wonder we become spiritually exhausted!

Make a decision today to pare down your obligations and to streamline your schedule.

Too Much Baggage An old axiom of traveling is this: put everything you think you'll need or use into your suitcases and then take out half of what you've packed. The point is that most of us take along too much stuff when we travel.

The same principle holds true in life. Most of us have acquired too much baggage, and lugging it is wearing us out and depleting us of spiritual resources.

Lighten the Load None of us can have it all, do it all, know it all, or be it all.

- Ask the Lord to guide you as you evaluate the commitments you have made and to reveal to you which ones He wants you to lay aside.

- As He leads, look for what you might subtract from your daily schedule.

- Look for what you might subtract from your overall schedule of life.

Be faithful to the commitments you make. But before taking on another commitment, talk to the Lord about it. Don't feel that you must do everything others ask you to do.

Add by Subtracting   In subtracting one thing from our list of duties, chores, and tasks, we often find that we are adding One. We'll likely discover that we are more relaxed in our prayer lives and feel a greater desire to spend more time in intercession. We are more likely to devote longer periods of time to reading His Word and meditating on it. By eliminating a time-demanding obligation, we often feel more free to spend time with the Lover of our souls.

Not only are we setting down a burden when we subtract one from our lives, but we are also taking up a renewed relationship with the Lord. And in that there's always spiritual renewal!

33 ✳ Choose to Give

Giving is a conscious act. It doesn't happen by chance. It usually isn't our first response. Giving is a deliberate act of setting aside self and focusing our time, attention, and resources on others.

Giving that lifts us up spiritually is—

- *An act of joy.* Give with joyful expectancy about what the Lord is going to accomplish through your giving. Give with the expectation that your giving is going to make a difference.

- *An act of the will.* Don't give because you feel manipulated to give or obligated by others to give. Give of your own volition, not grudgingly.

- *Aimed.* Make your giving purposeful. Aim it where you truly believe it will bear the most fruit for the gospel's sake. Seek to accomplish something with your giving. Invest your giving in anticipation of a good return to the Lord's account.

Claim God's Blessing   In focusing your giving, you'll no doubt also have an inner assurance that you are truly a partner with the Lord in accomplishing His purposes on the earth. The giving you plant into God's work will be multiplied and used by God to bear fruit, and you personally will have what you need in abundance and will feel an abundance in your spirit at the same time.

Giving frees us from a vicious struggle for possessions and from a debilitating preoccupation with calculating how to gather more material things for our own use.

A generous, thankful, joyful-in-giving spirit is a lifted spirit. Choose to give!

34 ✳ Give Consistently and As Much As You Can

Giving just once in a while can be spiritually freeing. Even more freeing, however, is developing a *life-style* of giving that is continual and consistent.

Make Giving a Consistent, Integral Part of Your Life   Jesus taught, "Freely you have received, freely give" (Matt. 10:8). Be a steadily flowing conduit of God's blessings, receiving His abundance and passing it on. Rather than making an occasional gift, become a consistently giving person.

Find a place where you can give regularly and frequently to the Lord's work. Ask the Lord to guide you in choosing that place. Then be faithful in giving to that work.

Give in a way that enhances the full ministry of the church. If your church doesn't help support an evangelist or a missionary, find someone whose ministry you can help support personally in an ongoing way.

Biblical Giving   Biblical giving is of three types.

1. The first type is the *tithe*, the tenth of all first-fruits, the *expected* return. This is giving off the top to

acknowledge that God has provided and that you expect God will continue to provide.

2. The second type of giving is the *offering.* This is giving our excess to the Lord's work. It's giving what is left after our needs are met.

3. The third type of giving is the *sacrifice.* Sacrificial giving moves beyond the expected return and beyond our excess into that which we actually need. It's giving up part of the very sustenance of our lives —taking a portion of the bare minimum and giving it away to benefit another.

Grow in Giving   Not all of us are capable of giving sacrificially—yet. We grow in our capacity and our desire to give, just as we grow in all other areas of our life in Christ. The key to a lift in spirit is to seek to give more than we are presently giving and to do so consistently. Set new levels of giving for yourself. Aim at giving more this year than you gave last year.

Choose not only to give but also to become a giving person. Your spirit may not be able to contain the blessings!

35 ✳ Give from Every Area of Your Life

Giving can take a variety of forms. Often we can experience a spiritual release or lift by giving from one area of our lives that we had previously withheld or shut off—consciously or unconsciously—from the Lord.

Look for Ways to Give

- *Give your money and financial resources, including investments.* Think of yourself as a manager of God's funds. Give Him a generous allowance even as you strive for the highest rate of return on His behalf.

- *Give your tangible goods.* Do you have excess? Is your basement, attic, or garage filled with things that could be used in His kingdom or that fellow Christians need?

- *Give your home.* Develop a generous spirit of hospitality. Open your home to meetings and times of fellowship with other Christians.

- *Give your time.* Find ways to give your time to those who know the Lord and to those who

don't yet know Him. Be a ready listener. Be
flexible and available to help in a pinch.

* *Give your service.* Ladle soup for the homeless
who may come to your church for a meal. Help
with hospital visitation. Help gather and dis-
tribute groceries to needy families at Thanksgiving. Use your van to take several homebound
persons to a church service.

* *Give your talent.* Are you good with a needle?
Help embroider new vestments or make needle-
point kneelers for the church. Are you skilled as
a graphic artist? Help in your church's printing
needs. Are you a carpenter? Volunteer to help
with the ever-present building and repair needs
at your church. Are you good at washing dishes
or sweeping floors? Your service is valuable
when rendered to the Lord!

* *Give your knowledge of the Lord.* Find an outlet
for sharing what you know about the Lord and
the Bible.

Principles of Abundance   In what areas
have you been particularly blessed with abundance?
In that area you are called to be the greatest giver.

Beginning to give in an area of your life from which
you have previously given nothing or giving more
than you have been giving opens you to receive more
in that area of your life and to receive more in *every
other area* of your life.

36 ✳ Be a Bubbling Fountain of Praise

Choose to praise the Lord all day. The psalmist stated

> I will bless the Lord at all times;
> His praise shall continually be in my mouth
> (Ps. 34:1).

The Nature of Praise

- Praise doesn't operate according to a calendar or a clock. Praise is appropriate anytime, anyplace.

- Praise isn't measured by the spoonful but by the bucketful from a fountain of never-ending supply.

- Praise sets us apart as God's people and establishes us as God's servants.

- Praise is an act of volition. We don't praise Him because He causes us to do so. We praise Him because we are created to do so and desire to do so. We choose to praise, just as we choose to pray. We can choose today to be a fountain of praise for the Lord.

Praise the Lord All Day Long

- *With our lips.* Praise is not thought—it is voiced! Praise is verbal and vocal. Praise Him as you drive to work, as you dust your house, as you mow your backyard.

- *With the words and symbols that surround us.* Wearing a cross can be a word of praise that sends a message to the world. A placard on your desk that gives praise to the Lord can lead to a conversation about Jesus Christ and thus act as an oasis to which another person is drawn.

- *With our behavior.* Our entire lives can be a praise song to the Lord if we continually reference Him as the source of our strength, the cause of our joy, the wellspring of our love, the object of our faith, the reason for our works, and the hope of our future.

Choose to be a wellspring of joy today and let your praises bubble forth in your words and deeds. You'll be refreshed, even as you refresh others.

37 ✸ Tell Someone About Jesus

Stop talking about yourself, your problems, and your accomplishments. Start talking about the Lord, and you can *count* on experiencing a lift to your spirit!

Talk about Jesus with Someone Who Seems to Know Him More Intimately Than You Do Ask your older brother or sister in the Lord:

- What is the most important thing you've ever learned about the Lord?

- How can I know the Lord better?

- How can I use my faith?

- What can I do to build myself up spiritually?

Talk about Jesus with Someone Who Knows Him in the Same Way You Do Seek out a friend who believes what you believe. Talk about the work of the Lord in your lives. Kindle faith in each other. Stir up the spiritual gifts within you (see 2 Tim. 1:6). Encourage each other to grow even more in your knowledge and understanding of the Lord and His Word. Pray for each other to experience more of the power and love of God flowing in and through your lives.

Talk about Jesus with Someone Who Doesn't Yet Have a Personal Relationship with Him

Always be on the alert for this opportunity. If you are living the life the Lord Jesus wants you to live on this earth—keeping His commandments, doing His work, and speaking the words He prompts you to speak—others will ask you about Him. Your very life will be a light that attracts others to the brightness and warmth of the Lord within you.

Tell Your Story

The questions that searching people may ask you are often like these: "Something's different about you. What is it?" "Why do you do that?" "Where do you get the strength to do what you do?" Others may come to you seeking advice or assistance about special problems they are facing.

When that happens, consider yourself summoned to the witness stand to be an eyewitness to the Lord!

What does an eyewitness do? He tells what he has seen or knows personally to be true. He answers questions under cross-examination as completely as he can but doesn't stray from the central point of his testimony. He doesn't feel compelled to be an "expert witness." He knows that his eyewitness account is the most convincing witness that can be given.

38 ✳ Seek to Make Only One Change at a Time

Many of us seek to revolutionize our lives at some point. We want a complete makeover, accomplished overnight. When that doesn't happen, we often become frustrated and give up on *any* change.

Adopt a New Approach   Instead of taking the all-or-nothing approach, try asking the Lord to redeem just one area of your life. Turn the spotlight of His Word on just one area of darkness in your soul. Trust Him to remove one sin, instill one new compassion, or resolve one difficulty.

If you feel that you must make a New Year's resolution, limit yourself to just one! Isolate just one goal to which you are truly willing to commit your time, energy, and resources. Set your sights on the long-range future but live your commitment to a new goal on a daily basis.

How to Make Changes in Your Life

1. If you want to see changes and growth in your life; begin with prayer. Ask the Lord to reveal to you the areas where you need to be forgiven, restored, healed, renewed, or strengthened.

2. When the Lord shows you an area of sin or

weakness, admit it and repent of it. Make a commitment of your will to turn away from that false belief, evil activity, or destructive association.

3. *Daily* ask the Lord to help you overcome evil with good—to replace your old thought patterns and behaviors with new ones that He gives.

4. Diligently search God's Word for His antidote to the problem. Focus on His promises to you.

5. Ask the Lord to quicken His Word to you so you will remember it each time you are faced with the temptation to revert to your old habits, ways of thinking, or associations.

6. Ask others around you to help you make the change you are seeking to make in your life. Ask them *not* to tempt you.

7. Ask fellow Christians to support you in prayer and to help you strengthen your resolve to live in a way that is pleasing to the Lord.

We are called as Christians to walk one step at a time and to live one day at a time. Trust God to give you a spiritual lift in *that* area.

39 ❋ Do the Daily Dozen-Dozen

Make a conscious decision that you will look for God at work in your world . . . that you will receive into your life the good that God is doing . . . and that you will be a source of good deeds and good words to others.

The Positive Side of Life   How can we do this in a very practical way?

Pursue the daily dozen-dozen! Try doing the following dozen things a dozen times each.

1. *Smile at a dozen people today.* Start with yourself in the mirror!

2. *Smell a dozen flowers.* Don't limit yourself to stopping to smell the roses. The flowers just might come in the form of perfumes and after-shave fragrances.

3. *Help a dozen people.* Help in small ways—holding doors open, picking up fumbled packages, watering the neglected plant of an associate.

4. *Read a dozen red-letter statements by Jesus.* Get a Bible in which the words of Jesus are printed in red. Read at least a dozen sentences attributed to our Lord.

5. *Take in at least a dozen pieces of positive news or*

information. These might include positive news briefs, information clips, or testimonials from the daily newspaper, a television or radio program, or a ministry-oriented or inspirational magazine.

6. *Look for a dozen scenes in life that give you joy.* Stop to look at the baby in the passing carriage. Enjoy the clouds passing overhead in the bright blue of the sky. Watch a squirrel gathering nuts.

7. *Stretch your body in a dozen different ways.* Thank the Lord that you are alive and able to move.

8. *Pray for a dozen people.* By name. For specific needs.

9. *Give affirmative words or compliments to a dozen different people.* Look for something about which you can give a genuine compliment.

10. *Give away a dozen hugs.* At least. To each child. To your spouse. To those with whom you have an appropriate hugging relationship.

11. *Praise the Lord a dozen times during the day.*

12. *Thank the Lord for at least a dozen different things.* Be specific.

Make It a Habit   Build your daily dozen-dozen into a habit. After a while these activities will become normal parts of your outlook on the day.

When the Burden Becomes Too Heavy to Carry

40 ✳ Ask for Prayer

When you are down, down-and-out, down in the mouth, or spiritually down for the count, ask others to pray for you!

Don't Go Solo   We were never designed to walk through this life by ourselves. God's plan is that we live not only in relationship with Him but also in relationship with other human beings who love Him and are of like mind toward Him—both to give to them and to receive from them.

- Jesus taught that when two or more are gathered in His Name, He will be in their midst (see Matt. 18:20).

- Jesus also taught that if any two of us agree in prayer on something that we ask, we will have it (see Matt. 18:19).

- When we ask the Lord, He will always provide others to help lift us up to a place of victory over the enemy of our souls (see Exod. 17:8–13).

Therefore, when you are feeling spiritually down, call on someone to pray with you and for you!

Call for Prayer When You Are—

- Sick or injured.

- Discouraged.

- Worried.

- Struck by adversity.

- Plagued by doubt.

- Stricken with grief.

- Struggling with bitterness, loneliness, alienation, separation, rejection, or temptation.

- Feeling the burden of intercession for another person.

- Weighed down by guilt.

No problem is too big or too small for prayer.

Who Can Pray with You   *Call on the elders of your church*—those within your own church body who are older in the Lord than you.

Call your friends for prayer. Prayer is petitioning. In the political arena, the more names on a petition, the greater the impact of the petition on the ruling authorities. Don't consider the prayers of anyone too small or too insignificant in your battle to regain wholeness.

Call the prayer line of a major ministry.

Prayer Tips

- Be quick to ask for prayer.

- Avail yourself of all the prayer help you can get.

- Open yourself to prayer. Expect God to hear you and answer you. Expect God to move on your behalf and to bring about His highest and best purposes in your life.

How should Christians spell relief? P-R-A-Y-E-R! It's the key to spiritual release.

41 ✳ Read the Miracles of the Bible

The Bible is filled from cover to cover with stories of God's miraculous intervening power. Read them! You'll come away with a sense that absolutely *nothing* is impossible for God.

Bible Miracles   Read the Bible miracles that tell of—

- *Healing.* Paralytics, lepers, diseased ones, the injured, the deaf, the blind, those with speech impediments, the withered and paralyzed, the crippled—He healed all.

- *Deliverance from demons.* Unclean spirits that maim, control, and alienate must flee!

- *Deliverance from circumstances*—flood, pestilence, fire, descending enemies, falling walls, prison walls, poisonous vipers, a shipwreck, a fiery furnace, stormy seas, a lion's den, or the belly of a great fish. God preserves and protects those who cry out to Him!

- *Provision.* A son in old age, wealth, water, a net-breaking load of fish, quail and manna, a debt-paying supply, fish and loaves, or wine—God always provides in a more-than-sufficient way.

* *Defeat of death.* Whether by raising people from it or keeping people from it, God demonstrates repeatedly in the Scriptures His power over death. Resurrection and eternal life are promised to all who believe.

* *Defeat of the unrighteous forces against our lives* —plagues, pestilences, punishments. God executes vengeance on those who countermand His purposes and persecute His beloved ones.

* *Revelations of Himself to humankind*—in burning bushes, pillars of cloud and fire, commandments etched in stone, a donkey that speaks, a rod that buds and bears fruit, angels who deliver messages, a vine that grows and withers, glimpses into heaven, words of prophecy, and Damascus-road-style interventions. God continually attempts to reveal His love to people through a multitude of methods. His miraculous methods are unlimited!

* *Forgiveness.* The ultimate miracle is available to all who request it with humble hearts!

How Good Can Life Get?   As grand and powerful and glorious as the Bible miracles are, even they do not depict the full extent of God's miracle-working power. As the apostle Paul declared, God is "able to do exceeding abundantly above all that we ask or think" (Eph. 3:20 KJV).

42 ✸ Intercede with a Prayer Partner

Find someone with whom you have great empathy of spirit and build a relationship that has prayer at its core.

Enjoin that person regularly for a season of prayer. Become partners together in the work of intercession—for each other and for others.

How to Intercede for Others

- Ask God to guide your prayer time. Express to Him your concerns, but ask Him to reveal to you His concerns too.

- Spend your time together in prayer. Don't spend an hour discussing a situation and then coat your discussion with sixty seconds of prayer. Make *prayer* the substance and the content of your time together.

- Maintain confidence about what you pray and for whom you pray. Often as you pray, the Holy Spirit will bring certain people, situations, or aspects of a problem to your mind that you may not have thought of previously. Keep those matters in confidence between you.

- Pray with expectation. Anticipate that God will act and that His actions will be 100 percent for good.

- Pray about everything that comes to mind in relationship to the situation, person, or issue.

- Pray until you feel released by the Lord. A moment of freedom will come when you know that you have prayed fully.

43 ✳ Repent

Experiencing God's forgiveness always brings a spiritual lift! The key to this experience lies in repentance.

Born Again!   Do you *know* in your heart without a doubt that you have a personal relationship with the almighty, living God?

If not, you can have such a relationship and be filled with His Spirit. Many people, including Jesus Himself in John 3, have described the experience as being spiritually born again—of moving from a spiritually dark, sin-constricting, and meaningless void to the light of spiritual revelation, freedom, and the breath of God. What blessed relief to be forgiven and to have an open channel of communication with the Lord God, through which you can repent and be forgiven on a daily basis.

Steps to Freedom from Sin   If you are struggling under the weight of unforgiven sin, take these eight vital steps.

1. *Face up to your sin.* Don't try to justify it any further. Don't carry the burden of it any longer.

2. *Choose to turn to God.* Don't run from God. Run

toward Him with your sin. No sin is too great for His forgiveness.

3. *Confess your sin to God.* He knows about it already. He wants to know that *you* recognize that you have violated your relationship with Him and have separated yourself from His presence.

4. *Repent of your sin.* Declare to God that your heart's desire is to be free of sin and not to engage in it further or again—in thought, word, or deed. Make a commitment of your will to turn from your sin toward God.

5. *Ask God's forgiveness.* The Lord promises that when we confess our sins and repent of them, He is always "faithful and just to forgive us our sins and to cleanse us from all unrighteousness" (1 John 1:9).

6. *Accept God's forgiveness by faith.* When you confess and repent of your sins and seek God's forgiveness, He forgives. Accept that fact. Furthermore, He completely obliterates the memory of your sin from His thoughts. He thoroughly wipes your slate clean.

7. *Ask for God's help in facing future temptation.* Invite the Holy Spirit to indwell your life and to give you both the strength and the courage not to sin.

8. *Go forward in your life.* Once you have repented and accepted God's forgiveness by faith, move forward. Forgive yourself. Forget what is past.

Nothing matches the spiritual lift of knowing that you are free of guilt and sin. It's the key to experiencing a spiritual lift in all other areas of your life!

44 ✳ Seek Out Wise Counselors

No one can know everything. Don't be ashamed that you don't know the answer to your question or the solution to your problem. Ask for help when you need it.

Choosing a Counselor

- *Choose a counselor.* Not everyone is trained in counseling skills. Many can pray with you and for you. Few are good teachers of general principles about what to do, how, and when. Still fewer are trained to listen compassionately to your story and give you wise counsel that will help you unravel your particular situation fully.

- Choose a *godly* counselor. Consult someone who is seeking to live his or her life in accordance with God's commandments, with purity and righteousness as defined by God.

- Choose a person of *faith*. Don't subject yourself to cynical, scornful counsel. Look for a person who will build you up, not tear someone else down. Look for a person who believes that your problem can be solved—fully, definitively, and positively.

Applying God's Law   God's law extends far beyond the Ten Commandments. He has established *all* the laws of the universe—the laws of nature as well as the laws of human nature. He has a principle intended to undergird and govern every procedure and method that affects your life. He has a law to help extract you from any problem into which you have stumbled blindly—and even from those you have manufactured! Choose a counselor who knows how to apply God's law to your specific situation. Consult not only godly men and women but also godly *experts.*

Fruits of Wise Counsel   Seeking out and following wise counsel provide a spiritual lift in three ways.

First, you'll feel strengthened by knowing that another person is helping to carry the load.

Second, you'll be encouraged and lifted up by seeing the forward motion of your life.

Third, you'll have a sense of release that God has indeed been your Healer and Deliverer.

45 ✹ Put Down the Burden— Literally

Find a way of literally casting your burden down. Give guilt, sin, trouble, or worry a material form. Then discard it!

What Burden Are You Carrying? What burden are you carrying? Has it reached the point of being intolerable?

Load a satchel with heavy objects (books or rocks, for example). Use a large purse, a backpack, a book bag, or a large, reinforced shopping bag. Fill it until it is heavy. Say aloud to yourself as you fill your bag, *This is the burden that I feel. This problem feels this heavy to my spiritual heart.*

Then carry that burden around with you for a while. Carry it until your body begins to feel the strain or ache from carrying it. The weight of a spiritual, emotional, or mental burden is causing the same strain on your spirit.

Come to the Lord in prayer at the point.

> *Heavenly Father, I need for You to carry the problem I've been carrying in my spirit. I can no longer suffer under the weight of it.*

Then unpack your bag!

Bearing Others' Burdens Many people feel justified in carrying a burden for another person. Some even feel that it is their duty. Not so! The Lord calls us to *help* one another carry burdens. If another person isn't willing to have you *help* carry his burden, you are under no obligation to carry it alone! In fact, your carrying the burden may keep the other person from facing his responsibility. You were not intended to carry the full weight of another person's burden.

Get Rid of Dead Weight We all are familiar with the term *dead weight.* Feelings of rejection by another person are dead weight to your spirit. So are the unforgiven, unforgotten hurts rendered by others. Worry, fear, and doubt are all dead weight, spiritually speaking. Each of these emotions, when unresolved, will eventually hold you back from doing all that the Lord desires for you to do. They will keep you down in spirit and will rob you of the joy and freedom the Lord desires for you. Eventually, they will cause bitterness and despair, which can eat away at your faith.

Get rid of the emotions that drag you down, hold you down, and eventually put you down permanently.

46 ✳ Ask Forgiveness of Someone You've Wronged

Few things can give your spiritual life a more immediate lift than asking forgiveness of someone you have wronged! Are you aware today that you have hurt someone? Call up the person and say, "I'm sorry!"

Asking forgiveness of those you have wronged isn't an optional activity with the Lord. It's a requirement for your own forgiveness! Jesus taught repeatedly,

> *If you forgive men their trespasses, your heavenly Father will also forgive you. But if you do not forgive men their trespasses, neither will your Father forgive your trespasses (Matt. 6:14–15).*

A trespass is just that. You have overstepped another person's boundaries. Ask the Lord to reveal to you where others have placed boundaries. Ask the Lord to make you more sensitive to the emotional and spiritual well-being of others.

Ask the Lord to reveal to you the things that you may have done to harm another person inadvertently. Even if your actions were unintentional, the pain the other person has experienced is real, and your relationship with the person has been breached.

Asking Forgiveness　　You may need to ask the Lord to give you the courage to ask forgiveness of another person. Pray for boldness. Ask the Holy Spirit to reveal to you the right time and place to ask for forgiveness and to give you the most beneficial words to say.

When you ask forgiveness, do so—

- *Out of the public eye.* Meet with the person privately. Don't grandstand in your apology or call attention to yourself to seek sympathy or goodwill from bystanders. The only exception should be if your behavior injured the person's public reputation. In that case your apology needs to be a public one.

- *Sincerely.* Don't say lightly, "Oops . . . sorry!" or take for granted the other person's forgiveness by saying, in effect, "You forgive me, don't you?" Apologize as if your own forgiveness by the Lord is at stake. (It is!)

- *With an offer to remedy the situation.* Do what you can to make things right. For example, if you've damaged property, replace it or repair it fully. Make full retribution whenever possible. Ask the person you've wronged what he or she would consider just compensation.

Once you have received forgiveness from the other person, do everything possible to restore your relationship and to move forward together. Don't continually rehash the past.

What if the person doesn't forgive you? Recognize that you have done what the Lord has required of you. You can't force another person to forgive you.

What if the person demands a compensation that is beyond what you are capable of remitting or that you feel is unjust before the Lord? Ask the person to forgive the debt! Ask for mercy. If he refuses, seek mediation.

Asking for and receiving forgiveness from another person take courage. You will feel release, however, when forgiveness has been granted!

47 ✸ Choose to Let Go of the Memory

Are you haunted by a memory of the past—something you should have done; something you should not have done; or something someone did that injured you in body, mind, or spirit? Sometimes even the memory of a past accomplishment or success can be haunting!

Forgive and Forget Forgiving is conscious, intentional, deliberate work. You may not feel like forgiving. Pray, "Lord, I forgive. Help me to forgive even more!" You may not find it possible to forgive a person—or yourself—fully in one prayer. You may need to pray over each aspect of a situation as it comes to light or as it comes to your remembrance.

Forgetting also is conscious, intentional, deliberate work. Often we find it nearly impossible to let go of the memory of a hurt, including our own past mistakes. As long as we hold on to that memory, we are in a state of grief about it.

What's So Bad about Grief? There comes a point when you must let go of grief or continually nurse the pain of it. Grief prolonged and unreleased becomes a perpetually open wound in the soul. As such, it is an indicator of your will *not* to be healed. It's as if you had an open wound on your skin and purposefully rejected all attempts at medicating it or bandaging it. Asking the Lord to lift you up spiritually and, at the same time, refusing to allow Him to bring healing to your grief work against each other! How can you experience healing if it remains your will to be sick?

Ask the Lord to give you a desire to forget and to help you forget. Declare to Him that the remembrance of this incident is grievous to you and ask Him to heal your grief.

Discard a Memory   At times it helps to assign your memory a tangible, physical form—and then discard it!

Try writing the name of the person or the deed on a piece of paper. Then crumple up the paper and throw it into a fireplace or a camp fire. Pray as you do, "Heavenly Father, this represents a hurtful memory that has been haunting me day and night. I discard it now in the name of Jesus. Help me never to seek to pull this memory from the ashes."

Or pick up a piece of driftwood as you walk along the beach. Etch the deed or the person's name into it with your fingernail and throw it as far as you can into the surf. You can do the same thing with a rock and a canyon in the mountains.

Or use a crayon to write the deed or the person's name on a small rock and bury it in your backyard.

Or build a sand castle on the beach or in your

child's sandbox in the yard. Let the waves wash it away or turn the hose on it.

Let go of the painful memories that haunt you and continually force you to look over your shoulder at the past. It's tough to move forward in life if you are continually staring in the rearview mirror at an incident in your past. Purposefully choose to forget.

48 ✸ Dance!

Have you ever danced before the Lord? Try it! Every person not only is creative but also has an abundant capacity for expressing creativity!

You Are Unique

- Stop to consider that you are probably wearing a combination of clothing today that is unlike that of any other person on the earth.

- You will speak a string of words today that has never been spoken before and certainly not in the context in which you will speak it.

- You live in a house that is decorated and filled with objects that make your environment completely unlike that of any other person.

- Taken as a whole, your life will be marked by a set of experiences, people, and environments unknown by any other person.

- If you chose to fill a blank book with a story of your own creation, you'd find that your work of fiction had never been written before.

- Your voice pattern, your fingerprints, your footprints, your genetic structure—every aspect of your being is unique.

What does this have to do with dance?

Your dance before the Lord also has the capacity to be unlike anything *anyone* has ever done before! (It will probably be unlike anything *you* have ever done before the Lord too!) Just as the Lord takes delight in your words and songs of praise and worship, He takes delight in your dance of worship.

Worshipful Dancing   Why dancing? Because it gives physical expression to what you feel deep within. Just as talking out a problem can help bring release and acting out a situation in role playing can help foster healing, dancing out a problem can bring a release.

How do you go about worshipful dancing?

Just begin! Close the drapes, shut yourself away, kick off your shoes, make sure you have on comfortable clothing that allows for movement—and dance. You may want to turn on praise music or sing your own praise songs. Begin to move to the music.

At first you may feel silly jiggling or jumping or swaying or twirling before the Lord. Do it anyway! It may take a while for you to feel comfortable in the rhythmic movement of your own body. Experiment with various moves. Some will feel more right to you than others. Go with those that seem natural.

Dance until you lose sight of yourself. Dance with abandon, your heart focused on the Lord and His glory.

49 ✳ Be Part of an Ongoing Sharing or Fellowship Group

Join or create a group in which you can have fun. There's a difference between a sharing or fellowship group and a group that is task-oriented. The difference can often be summarized in one word: *laughter.* Associate yourself with people who give you joy and with whom you can share a good, hearty laugh.

Fellowship groups move your individual ability to play to a level where others are involved. When that happens, loneliness melts away. Camaraderie begins to grow. A mutuality of experience begins to build. Memories are forged. And ultimately, friendship is built.

Meeting Friends   Where do you find such friends? Frequently, you find them in group settings where you all are members of the group. To make a true friend, however, often takes one-on-one contact. Get to know each other. Tell the funny moments of your lives. Laugh together. If there's no capacity for laughter, there's not likely to be much room for deep friendship.

You may meet people through a group to which

you both belong or through your shared interest in a subject or activity; but ultimately, your friends will be persons with whom you like to spend time simply because of who they are.

Make a friend, and you nearly always find that you are expanding a *group* of friends—that those you like are those your friends will like and that the friends of your friend will become yours too.

Plan times when you and your friends can be together—a party, an outing, an event, a trip, or even a task. Give yourselves a reason to get together and give place to your friendship on your schedule. Don't just assume that you'll be together. Shared, fun memories generally don't happen unless you help create the framework for them.

Spiritual Benefits   How does a fellowship group give you a spiritual lift? It's more difficult to be sad if everyone around you is happy. It's more difficult to be somber if everyone around you is laughing.

That doesn't mean, of course, that your fellowship or sharing group will or should abandon you in times of tragedy or crisis. Quite the contrary! They'll probably be the first ones to rush to your aid. To be able to cry with a friend can be as uplifting as laughing with him.

Friends feel sad when you fall into a pit. They also give you a reason to climb out of a pit. They help you make the climb. They cheer you on as you climb. And they rejoice with you when you come out on top!

You'll consistently be uplifted in your spirit by the presence of your friends in your life.

50 ✵ Choose to Rejoice!

"Fear not! Rejoice!" That phrase appears frequently throughout the Bible. Actually, it is a *command*. Let's choose to obey it!

How Do We Live in Joy?

1. *We continually look for the Holy Spirit to invade all situations and circumstances of our lives.* We anticipate His help. We continually claim with our faith and proclaim with our praise that His supernatural help is on the way toward us!

2. *We exult in His presence when He arrives on the scene.* As in the case of the shepherds outside Bethlehem two thousand years ago, sometimes the presence of the Lord is so glorious, so sudden in its appearance, or so dramatic that we are stunned, awed —and even afraid—of His arrival in our midst. Rejoice! Choose to be thrilled at His presence, overwhelmingly happy at His arrival, and completely open to His working.

The Formula for Rejoicing

Praise. Relax. Praise. That is the basic formula for rejoicing.

We are to praise the Lord at the outset of a crisis or at the beginning of a segment of our lives.

Then we relax in our faith. We watch the work of the Lord as it unfolds.

We praise Him again as the crisis is resolved, the task is completed, or we move to the next phase of our life.

Rejoice Continually
Rejoicing is intended to happen on a continual basis. We should continually applaud the Lord's presence in our lives and the completed work of His hands.

Fear and joy are like two sides of a coin. Choose to live on the side of joy! Choose to rejoice—to praise, relax, and praise—in never-ending rhythm.

51 ✳ Pray Until You Get an Answer

Don't give up too soon in your prayer about a particular matter. Persist in prayer until you get God's answer.

Persistence in Prayer   Time and again we read stories in the Bible about kings, prophets, priests, and judges who, when troubled or surrounded by trouble, fell on their faces before God and refused to get up until they had full assurance that God was acting on their behalf or that God had revealed to them the actions He desired them to take. We should do no less.

Are you troubled today about the direction you should take in your life? Are you plagued with self-doubt? Are you weighed down with "decisions, decisions, decisions" that clamor for resolve? Are you frustrated because you don't know what to do with your frustrations?

Take your problem to the Lord in prayer and stay there until He answers you. Refuse to move until you know how He wants you to move. Refuse to take action until you're sure that it's the action He desires for you to take and that the timing for such action is right.

Fasting is rooted in this concept of persistence. We tend to think of fasting as skipping a meal and then praying about a matter that we consider important. The activities are right, but the emphasis is backward. True fasting is being so intent on praying about a matter that a mealtime comes and goes without our having noticed!

To fast and to pray mean praying with such perseverance that we remain in prayer without regard to the clock. We pray so intently and with such focus that we are oblivious to everything else around us— including, in many cases, our physical needs.

The Heart of the Matter   The real question is not whether we want God's answer to a problem. The question is not whether we want God's help, His guidance, or His intervention. The real question is how *much* we want God's solution to our problems, His presence in our lives, and His victories to occur.

Many of us leave God's throne room just moments before He whispers His answer in our ears . . . just moments before He causes the miracle to unfold before our eyes . . . just moments before we know without a doubt that He is in us, with us, for us, and about to work through us.

Prayer calls for us to be on God's timetable, not for Him to adjust to ours.

Care enough to *persist* in prayer. You won't be disappointed; you won't be denied. Rather, you'll experience more of His presence and see more of His miracles than you ever thought possible.

52 ✴ Stand Still and Ask for God's Peace

When problems seem so overwhelming that you feel as if they are going to capsize your boat, don't throw yourself into a frenzy of bailing water. Stand still and use your faith. Rebuke the winds and waves that are threatening to destroy your life and ask the Lord to give you His peace. (Read Mark 4:35–41.)

Stand Still

- Don't run to and fro across the face of the earth in search of an answer. Stand still and ask the Lord for *His* answer.

- Don't rush about trying to solve things on your own. Stand still and ask the Lord to move on your behalf.

- Don't hurry in and attempt to fix things according to your own understanding. Stand still and ask the Lord to guide your steps.

- Don't tell everyone or consult everyone within earshot. Stand still and ask the Lord to show you to whom you should turn and from whom you should seek counsel.

- Don't throw yourself into a tizzy trying to side-step the devil. Stand still and ask the Lord to rebuke the enemy on your behalf even as you resist him. (The Bible says that he *must* flee when you do that! See James 4:7.)

- Don't run in circles. Stand still and ask the Lord to point out His way.

- Don't wring your hands in despair. Lift your hands and stand still before the Lord. Ask Him to pour His healing, loving, calming, powerfully strengthening presence through you.

Ask the Lord to Supply Your Needs

- If you need healing, ask Him for it.

- If you need wisdom, ask Him for it.

- If you need love, ask Him for it.

- If you need encouragement, ask Him for it.

- If you need ideas, ask Him for an outpouring of His creativity.

- If you need provision—money, food, clothing, shelter, material goods—ask Him for it!

- If you need strength to endure, ask Him for it.

- Whatever you need that is useful or right according to His commandments, ask Him for it!

He promises to give you every good and perfect gift in abundance. He *won't* help you sin or self-destruct. He *will* bring you toward wholeness.

Ask for God's Peace   Above all, ask the Lord for His peace. Ask Him to soothe your wounded heart and to settle your troubled mind.

Make your requests known to Him in faith (with prayer and thanksgiving), "and the peace of God, which surpasses all understanding, will guard your hearts and minds through Christ Jesus" (Phil. 4:7).

Need a spiritual lift? Ask the Lord to give you one.

He will do it! In His way, in His timing, for His purposes . . . and always in His love!

Jan Dargatz is also author of *52 Simple Ways to Tell Your Child "I Love You"* and *52 Simple Ways to Build Your Child's Self-Esteem and Confidence.* She holds a doctorate in education from the University of Southern California, Los Angeles. She has traveled to more than thirty countries in the course of her work.